Seeking **TRUTH** is good.

Knowing **TRUTH** is better.

Applying **TRUTH** is best.

Contents

ABOUT THE AUTHOR 3
ACKNOWLEDGMENTS 5
THE EPISTLE 7
      by John E. Perry born June 5, 1942 7

A NEW BEGINNING 23
A NEW PLATEAU 33
A TUTOR APPEARS 41
FINAL REVELATION 53
APPENDIX 57
      THE TRUTH WILL SET YOU FREE (John 8:32) 57

MY TESTIMONY OF THE BOOK OF MORMON 69
MY TESTIMONY OF THINK AND GROW RICH 73
      "Helping dispel the Mormon misconceptions" 77

FAITH 83

For over a decade, John very ardently sought the truth. When he started searching he was 26 years of age and was working as an overhead crane operator in a nickel alloys factory. A unique experience in his life inspired him to be diligent in seeking truth. His quest caused him to go through many difficulties, including going completely financially destitute while having a wife and four sons to support. These difficulties gave him a unique insight into things as they really are. John learned the school of hard knocks is a very good teacher as we go through, not get stuck in, difficult circumstances.

The author daily studied, pondered and prayed many hours in his search for truth. He hopes his unique experiences will radiate with the reader, a thought provoking experience, as this book is read and pondered upon. In this essay, hidden in the journey, lay keys which are simple to use. These keys are so powerful they have the ability to open many glorious doors and can jettison anyone who embraces them to a richer and more peaceful walk with our creator.

ABOUT THE AUTHOR

John E Perry graduated from Barboursville High School in 1960. He attended Marshall University, majoring in International Political Science, Communication and Economics. He also attended The American College majoring in Estate Planning. He graduated from The Law of Success International. John worked for Prudential Insurance and Financial Services for 28 years both as a representative and manager. He had the privilege of taking many 3 and 5 day seminars, from highly trained successful people that added greatly to his reserve of knowledge for his profession and life itself. He was an adviser for The Estate Plan, the nation's largest provider of Revocable Living Trust. While a representative with Prudential he served as Vice President, and Union Steward of AFL-CIO International Insurance Workers of America for West Virginia, and part of Ohio.

John started Perry Investment Properties (PIP), a Real Estate Investment Company in 1970, as a hobby. He is presently CEO of Perry Investment Properties, LLC now a family owned multi-million dollar corporation.

The author has been married for 60 years and has 6 sons, 15 grandchildren and 24 great grandchildren. For the past 35 years he has been active in his church serving many callings; including, Ward Clerk, Mission Leader, High Priest Group Leader, High Council, Sunday School President, Councilor to the Mission President, Priesthood Executive Committee, and Regional Public Relations Council, just to name a few.

ACKNOWLEDGMENTS

I give special gratitude to Doctor Lisle G. Brown curator of Special Collections in the Marrow Library at Marshall University for inspiring me to write this Epistle. On several occasions in the past several years Lisle has suggested I write a history of some occurrences in my live. Lisle passed to the other side at the age of 69. He was a dear friend and is greatly missed. I appreciate Sarah Perry, my dear friend and granddaughter in law who graduated from Ohio University with a degree in English for her assistance in helping with editing. I am grateful for Sarah Martin, an English Professor at Marshall University for her willingness in assisting with editing. I express special gratitude and appreciation to my dear eternal companion, Cookie, for her willing heart in helping with this work. I also acknowledge our six sons who has taught me much about joy and heart ache, happiness and sadness, responsibility and accomplishments. My eternal companion and our six sons has added greatly to form me into the person I am. They have unquestionably inspired me to reach deep inside and discover how to progress in this station we call life. I acknowledge many shortcomings and deficiencies in my life and also acknowledge "hidden" inside of our shortcomings and deficiencies, are jewels of knowledge that allows us to progress if we embrace them properly.

The Epistle

by John E. Perry born June 5, 1942

The original purpose for writing this epistle was to pass this history on to my posterity; however, whomever this epistle falls upon, is welcome to read it, with the hope that it might edify the soul. The contents herein is derived from records, and personal memory or that which has been relayed to me from others, including my Mother.

June 3, 1942, at my uncle Otho Perry's residence in the 3500 block of Crane Avenue in the town of Huntington, County of Cabell, and the State of West Virginia, my Mother, Sara Ellen (Coffman)

Perry, was great with her fourth child being a few days into the eight month of her pregnancy. While walking on a brick walk in the back yard, a cow grazing nearby mooed, causing her to slip and fall, landing with her stomach on the edge of the brick walk.

June 5, 1942, 8:20am; Sara had prematurely delivered her six pound three ounce child at Saint Mary's Hospital. He was born blue and his heart was twice as large as normal. The Doctor thought the fall must had bruised his heart. The prognosis of her new born was not a very good one, and his condition was getting worse. A Nun came to her bedside informing her how ill her new baby was and that he may not live. She prayed with great humility for many hours, pleading with Heavenly Father to help our family Doctor. She vowed to Heavenly Father, if he would allow her son to live and be healthy, she would do all she could to raise him to serve Jesus Christ. After the Doctor worked with him for many hours his condition improved. A second X-ray was taken; his heart was normal!

The doctor said the earlier X-ray must had been misread for swelling couldn't go down that quick. This was the first vow Mother had ever made with Heavenly Father, nor did she ever make another. She passed on to the other side a month before her 97th birthday.

Around my age of five or six, while sitting on our couch in the living room with my older brother Daniel, we were having a discussion concerning tying my shoe. I was asking Jesus to tie my shoe, and Danny did not believe that Jesus would tie my shoe. I was sure he would. Mother was listening from the other room with a chuckle in her heart. As this discussion continued she entered the room, knelt down in front of me and tied my shoe, explaining to us that Jesus had helpers to assist him in accomplishing his chores, and that she was Jesus' helper. After she said that I looked at my brother, with a big smile on my face, saying: "I told you Jesus would tie my shoe." Mother left the room with a chuckle still in her heart.

My brother Daniel was 20 months older than I. Growing up we slept in the same bedroom in twin beds. Every night, before we climbed into our beds, Mother would kneel, Danny and I on either side, and we would say this prayer "Now I lay me down to sleep. I pray the Lord My soul to keep. If I should die before I wake. I pray the Lord my soul to take". On many occasions, when I was grown that prayer would come to mind as I lay in bed before I fell to sleep.

The vow Mother made the night of my birth inspired her to be steadfast concerning church attendance, especially Sundays. Many times she would not feel like getting her children ready and walking two blocks to Church, especially when it was cold and maybe snowing or raining. However, she felt that Heavenly Father had keep his part of the vow, by healing her son, and she needed to keep her part.

We faithfully attended Riverview Methodist Church after I was born, until my age of 14. Little lapel pins were given for perfect attendance. Even today in a small box in my drawer are some of those pins. One of the pins was for three years without missing a Sunday. A couple of weeks before my fourteenth birthday, our church held a revival that lasted a week. Nearing the end of the revival, I was actually listening to the sermon. While I do not recall the exact message, I do recall my heart pounding, when at the end, the preacher made an alter call for all who wanted to accept Jesus Christ as their savior. My heart was beating so fast I thought it was going to come out of my bosom. I had a desire to go to the altar and surrender my heart to Jesus Christ; therefore, after the continued beating, I seemed to get up enough nerve to walk to the front and commit my life to Christ. I had never experienced that kind of feeling before. Within the next week or so, all who had accepted Christ were taken to a Methodist Church on the corner of 31st and 4th Avenue to be baptized. Our church did not have a baptismal font and Reverend Shy wanted to baptize us by immersion.

Around age fourteen, I received a job delivering morning newspapers. Seven days a week I arose at 5am, traveled six blocks on my bicycle, and prepared the papers for delivery. I then traveled many blocks riding my bicycle and delivering the papers. My route started on 5th Street in Altizer and ended on 12th Street. Also thrown in on this route was a road on the other side of the tracks named Lawson Court. I learned that the early morning was the most beautiful part of the day. Snow, rain, cold or warm it was very beautiful and peaceful.

Friday evenings, I collected from my customers the money for the newspapers they had received. Ninety nine percent of my customers paid cash. I was busy with the paper route and do not recall going to church very often after I started delivering papers. I delivered papers for about 2 years.

The paper route was very close to a Dairy Bar where teenagers would hang out. They sold hot dogs, hamburgers, ice cream, candy and soda. The juke box and pin ball machines added to making it a great place to hang out. I entered the place many times over the next few years. About age fifteen, I would go there on Friday and Saturday evenings to dance and hang out. On many occasions, the place was so full that many patrons would have to stand outside. The juke box would play and many danced.

Learning to dance at fifteen was a lot of fun. This is where I met Lorna Ilene (Cookie) Matthews my future sweetheart and future wife. Sometimes she and I would dance the evening away. At my age of 16, Cookie and I decided to get married. March 21st 1959 Cookie's Mother, Leola Matthews, and her boyfriend, Perk Bellomy, drove us to the Cattlesburg Kentucky Court House, and assisted us in getting a marriage license. Near the courthouse was a small Methodist Church. The witness' to our wedding were Cookie's Mother, her Mother's boyfriend, who she later married, the Reverend who performed the marriage, his wife, and the custodian of the church. My parents were surprised to learn of our marriage about six or eight months after the occasion.

Marriage in the 11th grade, and living at home, Cookie lived with her sister, did not seem to change my normal routine. My expenses were still taken care of by my parents. Soon Cookie became pregnant. Then everything changed. Employment was not an option; it was a necessity. I was now responsible to pay for raising a family. The first employment I had, other than shoveling snow, raking leaves, passing newspapers or working as a caddy at the Guyan Country Club, was working at the Exon Service Station, located on the corner of Rt 60 and Roby Road. Soupy was the managers name, pay was 50 cents an hour plus commissions on items such as wiper blades, radiator caps, tires etc. that I sold.

The summer before starting 12th grade at Barboursville High School, I landed a full time job as a service station attendant at Carroll Trucking Company, making a whopping $1.00 per hour! I fully realized, that working full time, and going to school, while raising a family would be a challenge, therefore; I rehearsed my situation with a teacher at school. Thankfully, I had already taken some of the more difficult classes such as Algebra, Geometry and Latin. It was determined I could go to school a half day and still earn enough credits to receive a Diploma. In my senior year, I reluctantly chose easy classes such as general math instead of precollege classes.

My employer scheduled me to work almost every Friday, it was usually their busiest day. Other days worked were evenings and the midnight shift on Saturdays and Sundays. Working during the day on Friday's caused me to miss most of my English tests. Ms. Hertig, my English teacher, gave most of her tests on Fridays. The last three days of school were called class days, most students did nothing but visit with each other. However, I stayed in English class taking tests all three days. Twelfth grade English was a required subject and I had missed most of the tests. My grade was an I for (incomplete) and every test missed had to be taken.

Eleven days before our first wedding anniversary being the 10th day of March 1960 our first son, John Edward Perry II was born. Three months after his birth was graduation. Our graduating class wore white robes and white caps. Pictures were taken of John and I wearing my white graduation robe.

Upon graduating from High School and determining $1.00 per hour would not be sufficient to raise a family, my priority was seeking better employment. The economy, in our area, was very bad and better employment I could not find. My older brother David had moved to Florida and found employment working for a contractor. Their main business was building new roads. The pay was considerably more than what I was making. David had talked to the owner securing a job if I so chose; therefore, we decided to move to Florida.

In December 1960, we packed all of our earthly belongings into our car and a six by eight foot trailer covered with an old blue tarp, poorly tied down with an old rope, and began our journey south. Upon leaving snow was falling. Some had accumulated on the road. We did not realize it was the beginning of a snow storm. By the time we traveled to Charleston, WV the roads were very hazardous. As we proceeded to enter the West Virginia Turnpike we were turned away at the toll booth because, we had no chains on our tires. We drove back to Charleston, purchased a set of chains, and proceeded south. The steep hills and sharp curves of the turnpike made it extremely hazardous, even without snow. At that time the 88 miles of the turnpike, was considered the most dangerous major highway in America. Cars and trucks were stalled, blocking part of the road. We witnessed several wrecks and many vehicles had slid off onto the berm. We drove for hours and somehow were never stalled. Looking back on our trip, I feel very fortunate we came through all of that snow, pulling a trailer, without any major hitch. John II was 9 months old. He sat and stood between us almost all the way saying bye bye, bye

bye. Cookie was pregnant with our second child, with an expectation of an April delivery date.

The weather continued getting better the further south we traveled. Arriving at our destination in New Port Richey, Florida the sun was shining and the temperature was great. My first job while working for Joe Levisicy was a laborer, mostly using a rake and shovel. Soon thereafter I was "promoted" to a dump truck driver. I didn't mind being a laborer; however, I really enjoyed driving the dump truck. We hauled gravel or shell used as a base for the new roads we were building. Sometimes we would need to back up for a few blocks. We learned to back up somewhat fast, looking only in the rear view side mirrors.

April 23, 1961, our second son William Carte Perry was born in Clearwater, Florida. About the time Bill was to be delivered, my Father called and said I had a good job at International Nickel Company (INCO) if I desired. The economy had shifted, and the company had called all of their laid-off workers back, and they were ready to hire additional workers. My Father had worked for INCO for many years and had discussed our situation with his friend, the personnel manager, Milleo Lapell. Mr. Lapell, knowing that I had a High School Diploma, agreed to hire me if I could pass the Physical Examination. He also agreed to put me straight to work; therefore, John II and I came back to West Virginia about a week before Cookie and Bill. She had not recouped enough to travel from delivering Billy.

INCO was probably the best company to work for in our region. Most of their contracts were with the United States Government. Many components for the space program were produced in the Huntington plant. Wages were some of the best in the region and seldom were employee's laid off. INCO had hundreds of applications for employment and they were hiring daily; therefore, it was advantageous to start employment as soon as possible. After working there for about a year, over 2000 men were under me in seniority.

Starting at INCO as a laborer was very different from starting as a laborer with Mr. Levicy. I started in the cold drawing department on the four to twelve shift, working inside, around many different kinds of machinery, including overhead cranes. The first week or so, my job was to sweep or clean up in the Cold Drawing Department. As jobs were posted on the board I would bid on the job which paid the most money. Usually, those jobs were operators of different kinds of machinery. The first job was operating the pressure tester, then 25 ton and the 50 ton draw benches, then the ten inch Me-dart and several other jobs. I worked at INCO a total of eight years before I resigned. The last two years, I was an overhead crane operator working out of the Electrical Department. Working out of the electrical shop, allowed me to receive higher wages. It also allowed me to operate almost all of the overhead cranes in the plant, making the job more interesting. The largest crane in the plant could lift 100 tons. The hook was about the size of a car. I enjoyed operating overhead cranes; however, some jobs required very little work and I did not like just setting in the crane or loafing. There had been times when I did not make one lift my entire shift. While working at INCO, I occasionally worked a second job. I sold family picture albums, stainless steel cookware or life insurance. At times, I would make more in a few hours than what it took a whole week to make at INCO. The extra income came in handy, especially having four boys that needed a home to live in, food to eat, clothes on their backs, shoes on their feet and on and on. We were blessed, for all of our necessities were met. We even saved some money that allowed us to purchase our first home at age 21.

A New Beginning

April, 1966, married with four boys, sitting quietly alone at home was a rarity; however, that is what I was doing. To my surprise! A great powerful spirit came over me, which caused a desire in me to go to my bedroom, kneel at my bedside and weep excessively. Tears poured out of my eyes as such the bedspread was dampened. This experience illuminated my mind in such a way as to cause within my heart a burning desire to go to church with my family. To my recollection, I had not been to church since I was a teenager, nor had I been thinking about going to church. As I was still crying, Cookie returned home from the grocery store and parked in our driveway. I jumped up from my kneeling position, and dashed to the bathroom to wash my face. I did not want her to see me crying. When she came in the house, I rehearsed to her what had just happened and this Great Spirit came again and both of us starting crying.

The next Sunday we attended Riverview Methodist Church. Soon thereafter we started attending Altizer Baptist Church, which was about 2 blocks from our home. The normal attendance was from 40 to 50 souls. After being there a couple of years, being in the month of April in the year of 1968, a guest preacher had been invited to speak in our assembly. The meeting room was nearly filled to capacity. The preacher delivered a stirring sermon. Never had I heard a speaker like him. His message illuminated my mind in such a way as I could see in our church divisions, contentions, back- biting and gossip. In closing, he called for a rededication of our commitment to Jesus Christ. He asked all who wanted to do so to come to the altar. I thought many would go up and rededicate their commitment to

Christ. Too my surprise no one moved. We then started singing a hymn called "I Surrender All", still not one soul moved. I bowed my head and shut my eyes and said to the Lord, "if I could do anything to help I am willing to do so". As I finished my prayer a clear powerful thought came into my mind, "if you take the first step I will do the rest". I was very shy and did not have the courage to go up front; however, I lifted my left foot and placed it in front of me. To my utter surprise, my other foot followed and I found myself walking to the front, seemingly without any effort. A great spirit it seemed had entered my being! Once I was at the altar still standing, facing the congregation, my arms just seemed to raise over my head and then lowering them until I was in a kneeling position. After the service most of the congregation shook my hand and smiled. The Great Spirit was still with me as I walked home. This feeling I had never experienced. It was as if I was walking in the air. My mind was clear and sharp and my heart was full of love. This was the greatest feeling I had ever experienced!

I did not fully understand what was happening; however, I wanted this feeling to continue for the rest of my life.

Upon arriving home, still in total awe, amazed on what had and was happening, I still felt as if I was floating in air. I retired to my bedroom where it was quite. While laying on my bed, pondering on the occurrence, I saw in my mind's eye the world in living vivid color. It was as if I was in outer space looking at the whole earth. A bright light radiating from a point on the earth, getting wider as it raised in the shape of a funnel or pointed cone. The thought came into my mind, "God is blessing the world". Immediately after this thought my whole body zoomed in, I was now looking over North America. I distinctly remember seeing the State of Florida protruding out into the sea and the Atlantic coastline toward Canada. I could see all of the United States and most of Canada, then another thought, "God is blessing America". I zoomed in again and could see the light protruding from what I surmised to be West Virginia. The thought then came to my mind, "God is blessing West Virginia". Immediately after that thought, I zoomed in again to what I thought was Huntington. The thought, "God is blessing Huntington". This zooming in process continued until the light ended up on top of my head with the thought, "God is blessing me", added to that with greater intensity, was the thought that "Jesus Christ was coming to personally reign on earth". This last thought was more astonishing. The thought that Jesus Christ was actually coming to earth to reign "in person" had never entered my mind! The entire vision seemed to take only a split second. I marveled with amazement as I continued to lay in bed pondering on what had just occurred.

I had never read the Bible nor did I know anything about visions. I was truly a babe when it came to knowledge about Jesus Christ, his church, or his doctrine. This vision caused me to have a great hunger for knowledge concerning Jesus Christ. I started feasting on the Bible with great zeal. Shortly after the vision, I quit my secure well-paying job with excellent fringe benefits and started working for Paul Revere Insurance Company, with only four weeks of guaranteed salary and then commission only. Needless to say, most who knew me well, including my wife, mother, and father, thought I had lost it, for giving up my secure employment with INCO.

As a representative for Paul Revere Life Insurance Company, I had no set schedule to work, nor time card to punch. My manager gave me total freedom as far as work was concerned. Little did I know, at that point, how valuable that would become? It allowed me to study and ponder the scriptures long hours without any interruptions. Many days, I studied for sixteen hours solid, reading, rereading, and pondering. I stopped going to church because what I was understanding, the church should be, it was not. In my quest for truth I studied with, Catholics, Christian Sciences, Jehovah's Witnesses, Lutherans, Seventh Day Adventist, and several others. I listened to televangelists such as Billy Graham, Oral Roberts, Rex Humbard, Jimmy Swaggard, Ernest Agensly, Morris Cerello and more. I also studied world religions including, Buddhism, Confucianism, Hinduism, and Islam. I joined The Masonic Lodge and became a 32 degree Mason. My hunger for truth was unending. All of the souls I studied with seemed to me to be very sincere and fine spirits; nevertheless, I was having a very hard time finding the true church. None I studied with were teaching the doctrines taught by the early church. For two years, I was relentless in my quest for truth. My focus was not on making a living. I couldn't help searching the scriptures. I made just enough money to barely sustain my family. Good wages and benefits at INCO, plus working on the side, where long passed. Upon leaving INCO, we had over $2000 in savings. Financially, we were doing fine. After two years of searching for truth, mostly feasting upon the Bible, my income was zilch. Our checking account was zero as was our savings.

Twenty eight years old, married with four children, and not enough money coming in to provide for my family. My Mother would put money into my pocket or bank account from time to time. I resisted her giving us money, insisting on her keeping a record so I could pay her back. Before we came out of the situation, I owed her over $1,000. I always believed this whole ordeal would somehow become a benefit in my life; however, it did not appear to make any sense. I many times pondered Romans 8:28, repeating it often in my mind, "And we know that all things work together for the good for them who love God for them who are called according to his purpose". I believed that verse with all my heart, even though I was financially broke, and confused spiritually. Many times I would feel as though I was lying face down in the mud with my hands and feet tied behind me. I had been tossed to and fro and had lost many battles with Satan. Each battle lost, however, gave me more knowledge about him and his wiles. I learned Satan is a liar, deceiver, and a disturber of the peace. Many times during this period, I was grossly deceived by him. I could write a book about the experiences I had with him during that period. I was sure that loosing battles was not losing the war. I believed the Bible and feasted on it. The scriptures clearly said, "God would supply all my need according to his riches in glory of Christ Jesus." I was in the forest seeing only the trunks of big trees. I believed someday I would be lifted above the trees and see the whole forest and the beauty therein.

A New Plateau

August, 1970, very broke and somewhat discouraged, I walked into Nick's News, a bookstore downtown, and began reading prefaces of books. I do not recall ever purchasing a book, except required text books when I attended Marshall University. As I was reading the preface of one of the books, this quite little voice within said: "read it". This quite little voice with great persistence continued saying "read it" over and over. I used my last dollar to purchase the book. I believe it cost one dollar. I took the little paperback and drove to a nice shady wooded spot beside the Guyandotte River. I had gone there many times before to read the Bible. I opened the little book and started reading. It was very edifying to my spirit. I continued reading until darkness came.

Driving home that evening, I pondered on what I had been reading. The next morning I began reading again. I could not set the book down until I finished reading it entirely. My spirit soared to great heights! As I read this book, I could see the principles being taught therein were the same principles in the Bible. I had feasted on the Bible for the past two years to such an extent I had almost all of the New Testament memorized. I had worn out one Bible, and the Bible I was presently reading was very worn and tattered. I was so taken by this little book. I read it several times in the next few weeks, even memorizing parts of it. The name of the book was "Think and Grow Rich" by Napoleon Hill.

This little paperback organized true principles in a way that I could put them to use. Before reading this little book, I was like a ship without a rudder or a clear destination. Applying the principles in the little book in an organized way changed my life drastically. In a very short period of time, I was selling insurance almost daily and receiving great commissions. In just a few months, I was back on track, providing for my family and paying my own bills. The principles were working so well I decided to take a correspondence course offered by "The Napoleon Hill Foundation" or "Law of Success International". It cost over $200 and took 17 weeks to complete. Two hundred dollars was a lot of money; however, I knew it would be a good investment. Occasionally, I purchased those little books and gave them to friends or acquaintances. For several months I studied, memorized and applied the principles in the little book. I was making more money than I had ever made. I was so focused on using the principles in Think and Grow Rich that I was not reading the scriptures nor praying as I had been doing for the past two years. I found myself progressing financially, yet somehow, I seemed to have an empty spot in my heart.

One evening, I had an appointment with a couple who lived near the Huntington Field House. When I arrived at their home they were not there. I had read in the newspaper about a preacher from New Orleans, coming to Huntington, to speak at the Field House. His name was Bob Harrington, they called him "The Bourbon Street Preacher". I had seen him on TV a few times and thought he was different and even funny. I decided to attend, since I was close to the Field House and my appointment was a no show. He preached with great power. The emptiness in my heart seemed not as empty after the service. My whole family attended each night thereafter until the crusade was over. Shortly after the crusade we attended Highlawn Baptist Church and within a few weeks we became members. I had decided that the true church was not on the earth; however, we had four young boys who needed the influence of a Christian church. Soon after we joined Highlawn Baptist Church the pastor and the deacons had a severe disagreement, causing the pastor to leave. About 300 members went with him. The pastor formed a new church and named it Fellowship Baptist Church, of which our family attended and became charter members.

During my tenure at Highlawn Baptist Church and Fellowship Baptist Church, I regularly feasted on the Bible. This was very edifying to my spirit. I was aware the church I was attending was not organized as was the early New Testament church nor did it teach the doctrines; however, I believed our children needed to attend a church with a good youth program. We faithfully attended for several years, then came a time when it was not edifying to my spirit to attend services. Reading the Bible during the week lifted my spirit. When I attended church, my spirit would be deflated. I could not understand what I was doing wrong. One Sunday morning before church, I knelt in humble prayer asking Heavenly Father to help me see what I was doing wrong. That Sunday the pastor preached on what he and his wife had done. My mind was enlightened with understanding and for the first time I could see pride working. Even though the pastor and his wife were fine souls, it seemed an enemy had interfered with their progression. He said they had accomplished much. Not them and the Lord. This caused me to reflect on how many of the more spiritual and humble members had left that assembly. As I was pondering on the church service, the thought very strongly came into my mind "Come out from among them and be ye separate saith the Lord." I loved those people. I did not want to come out from them. They were good solid souls.

I stopped going to any church and continued diligently studying the Bible. Knowing the power of the word of God and not going to church, we started having family Bible study each morning before the boys would go to school and some evenings.

Watching televangelist seemed to some small degree help me feel like I was in a church. They would preach much truth, but would also mix in philosophies of men. They were artful in speech and presented their message well. However, there were so many voices teaching different doctrines. As I was not assembling in any church, I literally feasted upon the Bible again, with much fasting and praying. I recall one fast lasting six days. I lost 18 pounds!

During this period much knowledge was received. I would feel very close to the Savior and then he seemed to be very distant. This yo-yo spiritual feeling was truly a thorn in my spirit. It seemed as though I was trying to hang on to God, but not feeling a real comfort or rest with him. Every morning before I left for work, I would kneel down and ask Christ for direction. Many nights I prayed for long periods of time seeking knowledge and a closer relationship with the Savior. I recall one period of time wherein I lifted up my heart and my voice every night for two weeks with great vigor even into the wee hours of the morning, often with tears streaming down my cheeks. I was seeking truth, understanding, knowledge, and a closer walk with the Savior.

A Tutor Appears

One morning in 1978, while kneeling in humble prayer. My mind was illuminated with a bright light. It was perfectly round about two feet in diameter. It appeared to be floating in the air about twenty feet from my person. The light was brighter than the noonday sun; however, it had a very calming and soothing effect on my spirit. The light proceeded to come slowly toward me until it fell upon my being. With great intensity a voice came to my mind saying "I am sending the Angel Moroni to you to bring you to light." This was very edifying to my spirit. In 1968 I had received a vision that had illuminated my mind and lifted my soul to great heights. This vision had a similar effect. As I stood up it was as if I was walking on air. I rejoiced with the expectation of an angel coming and tutoring me! I knew that soon I would find the truth that I had been seeking for many years with much fasting, praying and feasting on the scriptures.

Several days after this vision, while sitting at our kitchen table, our family had a wonderful experience. I had just finished teaching Cookie and three of the boys, a lesson about the miracles of Jesus. Cookie had a back ailment that had tormented her for almost four years. This aching in her back had been examined by two separate Doctors. They could not find the problem. She had a constant ache in her back and almost daily it caused her to cry. The consistency of this ache caused her to be very nervous and this became a thorn in all of our flesh. For the past two years she couldn't raise her hands above her head, it was to painful. At the conclusion of the lesson, I asked Cookie if she believed Christ could heal her back.

She said, she believed he could; however, she didn't know whether or not he would. I immediately said: "He is going to heal your back". I was somewhat surprised when I said that. We had many lessons and never had I said that before.

We all put our right hands together in the center of the kitchen table. I put my left hand on her back. During the prayer I recall saying: to my surprise "thou foul spirit come out from her" closing in the name of Jesus Christ. After the prayer was over I looked into Cookies eyes and to my astonishment big tears were streaming down her cheeks. I had never seen her cry as relating to prayer or even a powerful sermon. I then asked: "how does your back feel?" She replied: "it doesn't hurt." She stood up and raised her hands over her head and proclaimed: "it still doesn't hurt!" For almost two years as she would try to raise her hands over her head it was if a knife was being stuck into her back. We rejoiced in the Lord! The aching to this day has never returned. I believe it was Mark who said: "is that all there is to healing?" I replied: Yes, Faith in the Lord Jesus Christ.

A few days after Cookie's miraculous healing I was at my cousin, Clara Kelly's, house on business to collect an insurance premium. She and I started discussing things of spiritual matters. I rehearsed to her how Christ had healed Cookie's back. She then said: "our church believes in healing". I then told her about the vision I had a couple of weeks earlier, including the Lord sending the angel Moroni to bring me to light. She then said: "Moroni is a high angel in our church". When she made that statement I was astonished! This gave me a desire to investigate The Church of Jesus Christ of Latter Day Saints. Of the many church's I had investigated years earlier, I had not investigated her church. I was sure it was wrong for I had heard from the pulpit many times they were a cult. Knowing that Moroni was a high angel in The Church of Jesus Christ of Latter Day Saints had stirred my heart so as to give me a desire to investigate. Clara took my phone number and soon Brother Willard

Carico called to arrange a visit. After talking with Brother Carrico missionaries called and made an appointment, so I could learn about the teachings of the church.

At our first visit with the missionaries the entire family was present. This was very exciting to me. After the missionaries departed, I was somewhat discouraged. Most of the time they talked about Joseph Smith. I wanted to learn about Jesus Christ. The second meeting I did not want the family to meet with them; therefore, I met with them alone. After the second meeting I was still somewhat puzzled. The discussion still centered too much about Joseph Smith. Before they left they gave me a copy of the Book of Mormon and asked me to read it. I was somewhat hesitant until I learned it was the Angel Moroni who delivered the book to Joseph Smith. I knew the vision I had concerning the Angel Moroni was from God and surmised I must read the book.

As I began reading The Book of Mormon; to my astonishment, there was a war starting to rage in my mind! Thoughts rushed into my mind saying: this book is not real, it is modern English, it is too easy to understand, and Joseph Smith is not a Prophet. I was aware of Satan's wiles and knew I was in the middle of one. I continued reading. The battle continued to rage. After about 10 minutes, a total calm came over my person. I continued reading with great astonishment. The Holy Spirit was lifting the veil from my mind. After another ten minutes of reading under the calm, peaceful, influence of the spirit, I knew the book was true. My mind had become so enlightened that I could not set it down. My mind was sharp and clear, it seemed as if I was comprehending 100% of what I was reading. I read it from cover to cover in less than three days. I thought I had found the fountain of pure knowledge. After the vision I had received concerning the Angel Moroni, I actually thought an angel with the name of Moroni was going to personally tutor me. I did not realize he was coming in the form of a book. The principles taught in the Book of Mormon and the principles taught in the Bible go hand in hand, this I knew for I had read each with much prayer and fasting.

When the missionaries returned they were surprised to learn I had read the book entirely and testified of its truthfulness. I do not recall how many times we met after receiving the Book of Mormon; however, the discussions soon ceased. I thought they were teaching things that conflicted with the book they had given me. I could not understand about the God's in the Pearl of Great Price. Somehow I had misunderstood and thought that if Heavenly Father had a physical body that Jesus would not had been born of a virgin. I surmised Joseph Smith in fact had translated the Book of Mormon by the power of God and after that he had fallen into apostasy. I knew beyond a shadow of a doubt the Book of Mormon was true. I could not deny it! I had prayed and fasted many years for truth, and I was very humbled for what I had received.

The Book of Mormon was true and I knew it! I did not join the church; however, I wanted to share the book with others. I purchased ten books at a time and wrote my testimony in them and gave them away. I mailed some to several televangelist, Oral Roberts, Rex Hubbard and Billy Graham, to name just a few. One time I was inspired, to purchase an airplane ticket and travel to Orlando Florida where Morris Cello was holding a camp meeting in the Twin Tower Sheridan Hotel and personally give him a Book of Mormon, and testify of its authenticity. I gave it to him rather miraculously, in person, as he set beside of me on an airplane, after we left Orlando International Airport. After purchasing many books I was told by the missionaries that the Bishop asked them to stop selling books to me.

Our family had not assembled in a church for two years. During this period, we regularly studied the Bible as a family. Upon receiving a testimony of the Book of Mormon it was included in our studies. Cookie and the boys were not impressed at first nevertheless they accepted it with caution. Mark was dating Angel Navy who was a member of The Church of Jesus Christ of Latter Day Saints. One evening she was at our home when we were having scripture study. She was amazed that we were using the Book of Mormon and not members of her Church. After the lesson had been completed she asked if I would mind meeting with the missionaries. I said that I would be pleased to meet with them. Over two years had passed since I had received the Book of Mormon and, I had feasted on it much during that period. When the missionaries came it was my intention to bring them to light and help them to see the truth. One of the missionaries whose name was Elder Paul Jenks, was very knowledgeable and had tremendous faith. He also was artful with his speech. I was going to line them out concerning Jesus' birth. After a brief discussion He said: "We don't teach that". There were a couple of other things we discussed I thought was taught by the Church and each point I tried to make he said "we do not teach that". My bubble had burst, for I couldn't straighten them out. I had been mistaken on what I thought was taught by the Church. The first missionaries I had met with two years earlier were not nearly as knowledgeable as was Elder Jenks and his companion. Maybe my heart was not ready to receive additional light and knowledge two years earlier. After a rather lengthy and somewhat deep discussion about spiritual matters, Elder Jenks, knowing my testimony of the Book of Mormon, gave me a copy of Mormon Doctrine to read.

The day after Elder Jenks gave me Mormon Doctrine to read three of the boys and I were going to fly to Miami, Florida. Cookie chose to stay home; she did not want to fly. I had been fortunate enough to sell enough insurance and annuities to win a five day trip for the family. In Miami, the boys played in the hotel game room, swimming pool and on the beach most of the time. I studied Mormon Doctrine. To my surprise, I could not find anything in the book that I could disagree with. Furthermore I was being given additional light and knowledge and pondered it in my heart. Upon returning home I met with the missionaries again. They asked if I would pray about being baptized. I prayed and asked for a sure knowledge about the church. I believed it was true, but I could not say that I know it was true. When I had received the Book of Mormon two years earlier I also received a sure testimony. I could say "I know the Book of Mormon is true". I wanted the same testimony about the church.

Final Revelation

June 21, 1981 I was baptized and confirmed a member of The Church of Jesus Christ of Latter day Saints and received the gift of the Holy Ghost. I believed it was true; however, I could not say "I know the church is true". After receiving the gift of the Holy Ghost, Sister Bean, who was an elderly missionary serving in the Milton area said: Brother Perry, you will not realize what you have received for about six months. That statement sort of burned into my mind. I did not know what she was alluding too. Sure enough, in about six months her statement came back to my mind and I realized I had hang-ups that were gone. For six months I had been on rather spiritual high. No more yo-yo feelings: I realized that his spirit was with me constantly. This knowledge was sure and peaceful. I now knew that the gift of the Holy Ghost was real and very different from just having the influence of the spirit. I still could not testify and say I know the Church is true. I wanted to be able to say I know, yes I believed; however, I could not say I know.

April 18, 1982, I received the Melchizedek Priesthood by the hands of our Stake President, Allen Thompson. I had hands laid on my head, by a priesthood authority, several times before and was not expecting what I received on this occasion. During the ordinance a Great Spirit came over me filling my heart with joy as to cause tears too come into my eyes. I noticed upon opening my eyes most of the saints in the room also had tears in their eyes. Immediately after the ordinance, while driving home, tears began to flow. I thought I would have to pull over on the side of the road for my vision was blurred with tears. After arriving home I knelt at my bedside and prayed. Tears continued to flow for about 30 minutes. My mind was clear and sharp; my heart was full of love and joy! It was if I had been walking in a very large Golden Field of Wheat Ready to Harvest. I came upon a clearing, seeing mounds of pure gold and beautifully cut diamonds and many other precious stones of all kinds. It all belonged to me. The Melchizedek Priesthood I had just received was a gift from Heavenly Father, which I had been desiring for many years and really didn't know that is what I wanted. My whole being was filled with joy! When I stood up from prayer praising the Lord, it was as if I had become a new person. I can now say without a shadow of doubt "I know The Church of Jesus Christ of Latter Day Saints is true and the Priesthood therein is all the Church claims it to be".

My heart feels much lighter after writing this letter. I appreciate our beloved Stake Patriarch Lisle Brown, who was my first Bishop, for inspiring me to write this essay. On several occasions over the years he suggested I write a history of some experiences I have had. Somehow him suggesting that I write this letter, and me not doing so, seemed to lightly burden my heart. The light burden is lifted and replaced with joy. Doctor Brown, curator in Morrow Library at Marshall University, was a very special friend, passed onto the other side at age 69 in 2013. He is greatly missed.

January 5, 2010, I wrote for nine and a half hours.

January 6, 2010 I wrote for four and a half hours. After writing the basic letter many hours were worked editing. I give a heartfelt appreciation to my wife, Cookie, my "grand" daughter in law, Sara Perry and my friend, Sara Martin who is an English Professor at Marshall University.

                    Revised December 27, 2019

APPENDIX

THE TRUTH WILL MAKE YOU FREE
(John 8:32)

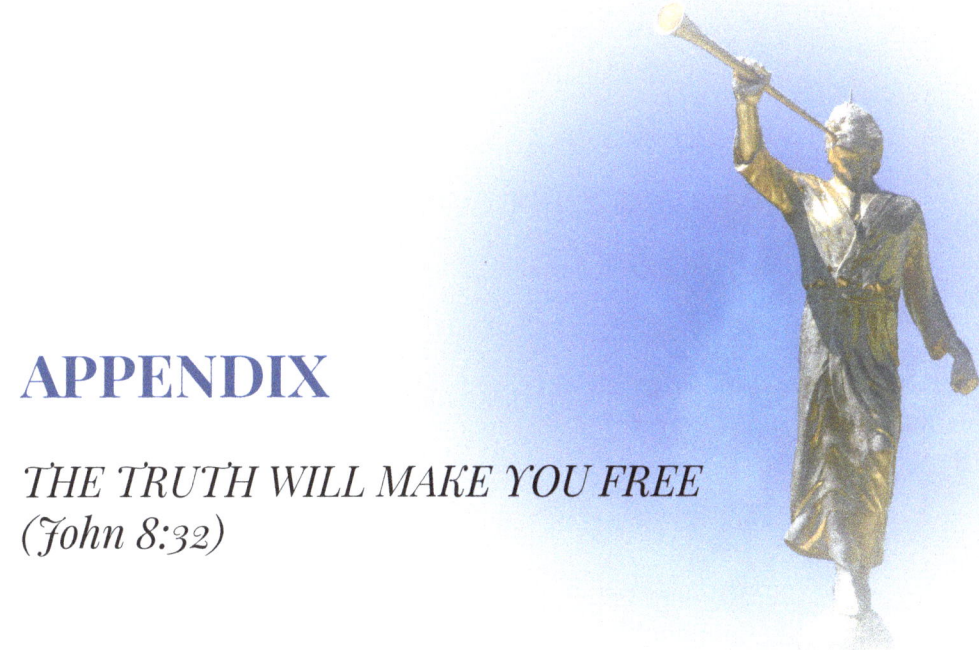

All truth is one eternal round. In the beginning was the word, and the word was with God, and the word was God, the same was in the beginning with God. The word become flesh and dwelt among us (John 1:1-2,14). Jesus Christ was with the Father before he received his physical body of flesh and bone. We also were with our Father in Heaven before we came to earth. We are literally" spirit sons and daughters" of a loving Heavenly Father (Heb. 12:9). We have a very special calling and purpose. Some heed the call and many do not. Just as Jesus Christ had to receive a physical body to full fill his call, we had to receive a physical body of flesh and bone to full fill our calling and reach our full potential. All of us received a physical body the same way, except Jesus Christ. His calling was so great that it required him to receive his physical body, being born of a virgin. He is the only begotten of the Father, Christ is also the expressed image of Heavenly Father's person (Heb. 1:3). Jesus Christ perfectly fulfilled his calling in every way and then went back to his Father (1 Peter 3:22) and received all that the Father has. Each of us have a major calling to become like Christ. His special calling made it possible for us become like he is. "We cannot do what he did", however we can be like he is. His character radiates truth and light. For us to become like he is we must develop his character (John 5:48). We must study and properly apply the principles he teaches (2Tim. 2:15). The principle of grace (Acts 15:11) makes it possible for us to fulfill our potential and receive all that the Father has (Rom. 8:17).

Paul speaking to the Hebrews in chapter four verse twelve: the word is quick (alive) and powerful, and sharper than any two edged sword. In Paul's day a two edged sword was the weapon of choice. Today our weapon of choice may be our laser directed bombs. Just how important is "truth" as we live in mortality? The truth, the word, the Gospel, God, Christ; all the same in this instance. Words are very important. God spoke and created the earth. What we say and how we process and interpret what we hear or read is "critical" in understanding truth. John defines the word as "God". The word and god are two words with many "layers" of meaning. More light is revealed as we seek, ponder and pray.

John said: the "word" became flesh and dwelt among us. To "fully understand" what John is writing may take some serious thought along with effort. We will get more light and knowledge as we ask God (Jam. 1:5-6) faith believing we will receive the "full meaning" of what John is saying. The most common way our creator speaks today is by using words spoken by his prophets.

Without the Holy Spirit we will not receive a "fullness of truth". The Holy Spirit (1 Thes. 1:5) will guide us into all truth.

God created man in his own image (Gen:1:26). Male and female created he them. Man in this case means male and female. Many times in scripture the word man means male and female. Male and female have by necessity different rolls in the creations, we can easily understand that by simply considering difference of our anatomy's, however in our creators eyes we are equal, walking side by side, for God is no respecter of persons. Equal does not always mean the same. All of us have a unique roll or calling in the creations and we all have the ability to "receive revelation from Heaven" to assist us in that calling. We are all spirit children of a very loving Heavenly Father, and are the most unique of all of his creations. We are the apple of his eye. All things were made by and for him (Col 1:16). Heavenly Fathers major purpose is to help his children receive joy (John 15:11). Peace, joy and happiness for eternity is the object of all creation.

Of all of Gods creations we alone are made in his image and are capable of having all knowledge and learning all truth. We can see things before they appear and then create what we see.

Knowing and properly applying truth allows us to fully understand the purpose of life and will keep open a direct line from our creator to "receive revelation", to know what truth really is (Gal. 1:12). A loving Heavenly Father has so created us that "we can and actually do", chose our own destiny. What we allow to be housed in our minds is of the "utmost import". Of all of Gods creations we alone have the capacity to "choose" what we allow to be housed in our minds. What we house in our minds eventually becomes our character (Phi. 2:5). The very reason we are to to strive to let the mind (words) of Christ be in us is so we can become like he is. We alone have access to all knowledge and can create many things. As Paul said, we can do all things thru Christ which strengtheneth us (Phil.4:13). The one thing we cannot do is atone for sin, again, "we cannot do what Jesus Christ did", however we can become like he is; indeed that is our calling and hopefully our goal. When that is accomplished we receive a "fullness of joy".

We are commanded to be perfect even as he is (Matt. 5:48). Jesus Christ perfectly applied and used the principles he taught. These principals are spiritual. We too can choose and apply and use these principles in our lives. That is how we can become like Christ. Learning and applying the principles he taught will eventually have such of an effect on our character we actually become like he is. Our Father in Heaven has never command us to do anything unless he provides a way to for us to accomplish the thing he commanded (1Nep. 3-7).

Faith in Jesus Christ is the first principle of the Gospel. Everything is matter, some is more refined than others. Some is easily seen and other more refined matter cannot be seen. Each of us have a spiritual body that is made up of a different kind of matter than our physical body. Our spiritual bodies left the presents of our Father in Heaven

(Jer. 1:5), to come to earth and receive a temporary physical body, so that we can be tested, and eventually we will receive a perfect eternal body of flesh and bone forever. Where we live or what glory (character) we receive is determined how valiant we are in learning and applying truth (1 Cor. 15:40-42, Rev. 20:12).

Jesus Christ is not only our creator, he is also our Savior. As we ask, seek and apply truth properly, here in mortality, "we are on our way" to eventually receive a perfect physical body of flesh and bone that will not be subject to sickness, disease, decay or corruption and a "fullness of joy". One does not have to wait to die to have joy (Rom. 14:17). We can and should have joy in this life, it is available to all who apply the plan now. His word in us provides peace, joy and happiness now. As one receives revelation from Heaven one KNOWS, and eventually receives a rest (Heb. 4:3) in Christ that cannot be expressed in words. "Truth revealed from Heaven" does and will set one free. We can have a rest (Heb. 4:3) and joy in our lives now, that surpasses all understanding (Phil. 4:7), even in tribulation (Acts 16:23-25). Our Father in Heaven loves to see his children progress. He continuously help's us along the way. There is a difference in joy and a "fullness of joy". A "fullness of joy" can only come after we receive our permanent physical body of flesh and bone and have been valiant in Christ. We will be able to run a six minute mile.

Learning to apply the plan including the principles is not an event, "it is a process". Line upon line, precept upon precept her a little and there a little until a fullness is received. The word of God is alive and powerful. As we commit to the principles of Christ and apply them in our daily thinking we are becoming more like him. Our thoughts should be guarded with precision (2 Cor.2:5). As a man thinketh in his heart so is he (Pro. 23: 7). Feasting on the principles of Christ daily, will increase our faith and will provide a shield of protection (Eph. 6:16-18) including artillery to ward off any incoming attacks that may be launched at us. Our battle is indeed more spiritual than physical. Our peace will be secure even in time of trial (Acts 16:23-25). Our faith will increase as we apply truth, we cannot fall, (Rom. 8:28)(Hel. 5:12) for we will win each battle whether it be great or small.

Learning and applying truth is just like every thing else that we may want to accomplish. It takes desire, commitment and persistence. There are many voices enticing us to follow them. There is only one truth. It has not nor will it ever change. Many however teach some truth, others teach some truth mixed with the philosophies of men, that can be empty and or confusing (Colos. 2:8). Not knowing and understanding the "full truth" or believing things that are not truth "will stop ones progression". Truth is revealed only to the humble sincere seekers of it. Only through personal revelation (Eph.1:3) does one receive a "fullness of truth." To receive personal revelation it takes personal commitment, (2 Tim. 2:15) humility and a sincere heart (2 Tim. 2:15). Personal revelation does not only bring us to KNOW the truth, it is also a way for us to live our daily lives and will draw us closer to our creator. This allows us someday to receive all that the Father has, even a fullness of joy. Only a sincere desire coupled with humble prayer and pondering relying totally upon the merits of Christ will one receive a "fullness of truth" thru the principle of revelation.

In the scriptures are some exceptionally special jewels that have had a profound effect on my journey seeking for truth. To fully appreciate and understand these jewels one will need much pray, pondering and fasting (Matt.6:17-18). There is no such thing as something for nothing, so it is with receiving a fullness of truth, it takes persistent effort. Ask and ye shall receive, seek and you shall fine, knock and it shall be opened (Matt.7:7). If ye like wisdom ask God and he will give it to you liberally and upbraideth not (means without restraint) (Jas. 1;5-6). In seeking Truth one must put their faith in Christ, not in man. Christ is truth and light and he desires his laws (principles) to be put into our hearts (minds). We know that "repetition" is a good teacher therefor "it is imperative that what we believe is really true". If one repeats a thing long enough in their mind, whether it is true or not, one will believe it is true. In my personal quest in knowing truth I had been taught and believed things that were not true, that was a stumbling block and had the potential to stop progression, it did cause much adversity. Faith in Christ coupled with desire and persistence will prevailed. I have learned that as one is seeking for truth there comes with that much adversity. It can even come from your best friends, however if one relies totally upon the merits of Christ truth will be revealed. A burning desire, relying totally upon the merits of Christ will prevail in receiving and keeping it. All truth is one eternal round and understanding and applying it brings great blessings including comfort, peace and joy to ones soul (Jas.1:25).

Following are some powerful scriptures if one prays about, ponders upon and understands will increase knowledge and Faith on their journey toward a fullness of joy.

Matt 5:48, 7:7 John 1:1-2 and 12-13, 8:32, Rom 8:28, 10:17, 2Cor 10:5, Gal 1:12, Phil 2:5, 4:8 Col 1:16 4:8, 2 Tim 2:15, Heb 10:16, Jam:1:5, Phil. 4:8. There are many other jewels in the scriptures as one ask seeks and knock they will find.

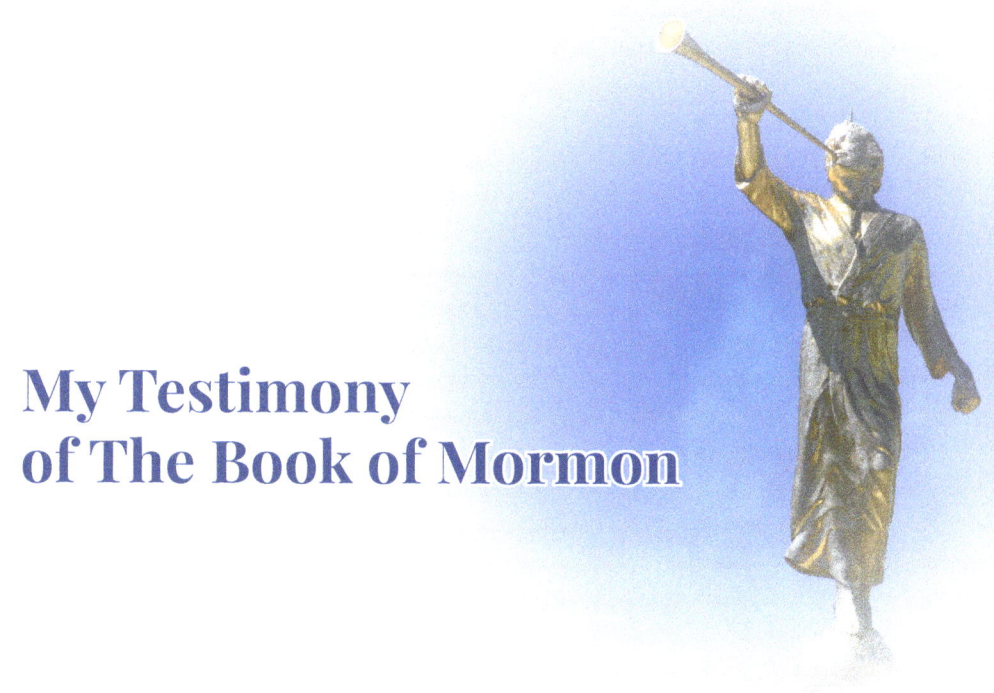

My Testimony of The Book of Mormon

The Book of Mormon has truly influenced my life in an extremely positive manner. After years of investigating many different churches and diligently studying the Bible, with much fasting and praying, I had the following experience.

In the year of nineteen hundred and seventy eight, as I was kneeling in sincere humble prayer. I saw in my mind's eye a bright light. It was perfectly round, and appeared to be about 20 feet from my person. It was very bright and very soothing to look upon. The light proceeded to come toward me until it fell upon my head. At that exact moment the thought came to my mind with great power, "I am sending the angel Moroni to you to bring you to light". With extreme joy I raised to my feet! It was as if I was floating in air. My whole person was edified with great joy! I had been studying, praying and fasting for several years for wisdom understanding and knowledge concerning spiritual things. I thought an angel named Moroni was going to come and teach me truth. I learned a few weeks later that a high angle named Moroni was highly revered in The Church of Jesus Christ of Latter Day Saints. For some strange reason in my quest for truth, as I investigated many different churches over several years, I did not investigate the LDS church. I now wanted to investigate. I needed to know more about the angel Moroni.

After my first discussion with the missionaries I was somewhat confused, for they talked about Joseph Smith most of the time. At the end of the second discussion, they left the Book of Mormon for me to read. I was hesitant to read it until I learned that it was the angel Moroni who delivered the book to

Joseph Smith to translate. As I proceeded to read the book, a great battle started raging in my mind. Thoughts bombarded my mind saying: this book can't be true, it is in modern English, it is too easy to understand and Joseph Smith is not a Prophet. I was truly in a battle with the adversary and I knew it. After struggling for about 10 minutes of reading, a feeling of total calmness came over my being. Within the next 10 minutes, I knew the book was true. I continued reading for several hours. It was as if I had 100% comprehension.

I was being brought to light and knowledge. The veil of confusion was being lifted from my mind and replaced with feelings of peace and awe. I know The Book of Mormon is a modern day miracle, right before my eyes. The angel Moroni truly delivered ancient writings to Joseph Smith who translated them, by the power of the Holy Spirit. This testimony has changed my life in ways that cannot be expressed in writing. I am grateful for the Book of Mormon for it has majestically enriched my relationship with Jesus Christ. My life, and the lives of many of my family, have been greatly influenced in a very positive way because of our testimonies of the Book of Mormon. Moroni 10:3-5.

John E. Perry **jep25705@gmail.com** February 21, 2013 I woke up at 6am this morning with a desire to pen this testimony.

My Testimony of Think and Grow Rich

"Think and Grow Rich" has literally changed my life in a very positive way. In August of 1970, I walked into Nicks News in Huntington, West Virginia, and stared reading in the self-help section of the book store. My eyes stopped on a "little paper back" with the title "Think and Grow Rich". As I was reading the introduction, a small still voice in my mind said: "read it", repeating the same words about 25 times before I purchased the book. The cost was $1. It was very close to the last dollar I had. Do to changing employment my income had dropped from $8,000 a year to $3,500 in the past 2 years. My present employment was based on commission and I did not have a pay check coming. Age 28, married with four sons and no pay check coming: you might say I was financially and somewhat spiritually broken.

After purchasing "Think and Grow Rich", I drove to a quiet place down by the riverside and starting reading. I could not put "that little paperback down". I continued reading and pondering until the sun set and darkness came. This caused my mind to soar with positive thoughts to greater heights than it had ever risen too! I had been studying and pondering the Bible very diligently for several years. Most of the New Testament I had memorized. Immediately, I knew the principles in "Think and Grow Rich" were true and Doctor Hill was showing me how to apply those principles in a practical way.

On the 22nd day of March 1971, I completed "The Philosophy of Success": a 17-week correspondence program offered by Doctor Hill. With diligence and persistence I started applying the principles. After many hard knocks, I was lifted up high above the forest trees" and could see the amazing beauty of the entire forest or this experience we call life. "Thoughts are truly Things".

I am presently a very young 77 year old and have been married 60 years. We have six sons, fifteen grandchildren, 24 great grandchildren and are continuing to be blessed in many ways, not excluding financial.

Applying the principles in "Think and Grow Rich" has expanded my mind in a way that not only allowed me to accomplish financial freedom, it has also greatly contributed to help me achieve "peace of mind" and an awesome confidence in our creator.

John E Perry Sr. **jep25705@gmail.com**

Revised December 27, 2019

The following article was written by John Perry, published in The Herald-Dispatch on February 2, 2012.

"Helping dispel the Mormon misconceptions"

Recently, I read an article in the newspaper with the heading "Here's a look at what Mormons believe." I'm sure the writer was sincere about what he had written. For said he, I've done considerable research on Mormonism. However, was his understanding correct?

I was raised in a Methodist church by a mother who loved Jesus Christ and set an excellent example of faith and good works. I knew nothing about the Mormon Church. An occurrence in my life caused me to study the Bible quite extensively. At age 28, I almost had the New

Testament memorized. In my quest for truth, I studied with many Christian denominations. I also studied world religions. I settled down in a Baptist Church, and continued studying the Bible with great zeal. I learned there are many voices in the world including but not limited to Buddhism, Islam, Confucianism, and Christianity. Christianity itself has many different beliefs, such as Baptist, Lutheran, Seventh Day Adventist and Catholic. This was somewhat confusing to me. All these different faiths seemed to conflict with the scriptures, Paul said, there is one faith, one baptism. (Eph. 5:5) One faith? Why are there so many different heads on Christianity? As a faithful member of the Baptist church, I continued to study the Bible with prayer and fasting (2Tim 2:15). At age 36, I had an experience that inspired me to investigate the Mormon faith. It was one of the few faiths I had not investigated. I had been taught from the pulpit that they were a cult. After much prayer, fasting and diligent study with real intent, I received a testimony of The Church of Jesus Christ of Latter-Day Saints. (Gal. 1:12)(Matt. 7:7-8)

Mormon is a nickname placed upon us by non-church members. The correct name of the church is The Church of Jesus Christ of Latter-Day Saints. Members and a few non- members use Latter-Day Saints or LDS as a nickname. In answer to the question are Mormons Christians? We believe the most important single event in human history is the atoning sacrifice of Jesus Christ (Col. 1:17-20). We try to live our lives in accordance to his teaching (Matt 7:24). Salvation comes only through the atoning sacrifice of the only begotten of the Father. President Joseph Smith said, indeed all things which pertain to our religion are only appendages to it.

Most Christians believe the doctrine of the trinity as accepted in the Nicene Creed of 325 A.D. The "majority" of the priests at that council voted to define the Godhead as: Heavenly Father, Jesus Christ and the Holy Ghost; with each being three distinct personalities in one body. This to many is considered a great mystery. The "minority" of priests at the council believed the three were separate in essence but co- equal. This caused friction in the camp of the believers. Latter-Day Saints believe the Godhead is three distinct beings with distinct personalities and responsibilities. We believe the oneness of the Godhead is in purpose, not in entity (John 17: 3-5, 21).

The King James Version of the Bible is part of the canonized scripture of the LDS Church. If all Christians interpreted it the same, there would be one faith; however, each denomination has a different interpretation. We believe the Bible is the word of God as far as it is correctly translated, just as other faiths believe their understanding is correct. For example, our understanding of 1 Cor. 15:29 differs from other faiths. In this scripture, Paul mentions baptism for the dead. We perform this type of baptism today. All Christians believe in the principle of proxy (one who acts as a substitute for another), Christ himself died for us by proxy. He took our sins upon himself.

We understand that salvation can only be attained through the atonement of Jesus Christ; however, we do believe that our works and actions reflect our commitment to our Savior. It is important to live your life in accordance with the teachings of Christ, not only to profess that he is the Christ (James 1:22). Only those who are valiant in Christ will attain their full potential (1Cor. 15: 40-42). Some of these works are the application of the following principles: chastity, honesty, humility, kindness, forgiveness, and alms giving (including tithing and service to your fellow man). The greatest attribute we can obtain is to have the pure love of Christ. Yes, Latter Day Saints are a peculiar people. We believe you will know a person by the fruit they produce (Matt. 7: 21-22) and that someday we will stand before Jesus Christ. The books will be opened and we will be judged by our works or by the fruit we have produced. (Rev 20:12).

This letter is not an official church letter. It is my way as a member of helping dispel some misconceptions of The Church of Jesus Christ of Latter Day Saints.

Faith

Faith in "Jesus Christ" is the crowning principle taught by our Father in Heaven. Without faith in Christ, it is impossible to please God. How does one develop faith? Repetition is a great teacher and a great way to develop faith. One of the precious jewels in Romans chapter ten in the seventh verse is "faith cometh by hearing". As we hear things we develop more faith in the thing we hear (good or bad) That is why Paul said in the second Corinthians to bring every thought into captivity (2 Corn. 10:5).

Repeating thoughts brings forth action which brings forth the object of the thought. Vocally hearing expedites the process. Writing down scripture is an act of faith. As we crystallize thoughts in our minds, we will "be drawn" to that thought and that will produce action. Faith without works is dead. In Proverbs we read as a man thinketh in his heart so is he (Pro. 23:7). It is our personal responsibility to bring every thought under control (2 Corn. 10:5). We determine our own destiny by what we think or by what we allow to be housed in our minds. How can we bring every thought under control? Learning and crystallizing truth will set one free. Heavenly Father has developed a plan whereby one can receive all he has, including a "fullness of joy". Keeping our minds focused on this plan we will achieve our greatest potential. How do we do that? We must fill our minds with correct principles. How do we do that? Study, pray and ponder on righteous principles. Write down scripture on a 3x5 index card, look at it often. Reading good positive books, watch good positive TV and movies or it can be a good computer game, listening to and singing uplifting songs and music. We have the privilege of putting into our minds what we want (Colo. 3:2). With freedom to choose (agency) comes responsibility and consequences. When Jesus said to us be ye perfect, he was saying for us to put into practice the principles he was teaching (Matt. 5:48). When we have mastered and applied those principles then we are perfect (complete) in Christ (truth). This is not an event, it is a process, we learn and apply them, line upon line, precept upon precept here a little and there a little until we are complete (Phil. 2:12). We are expected to "live the principles" not merely know them. We start with living the principles we know now. In the Sermon on the Mount many of the principles are taught (Matt. Chapters 5, 6 and 7). At the end of the sermon Jesus said: He who "heareth" these sayings "and DOETH THEM" I will liken him to a wise man who built his house upon a rock (truth) and when the rains fell and the floods came and the winds blew it fell not because it was built upon a rock "(truth"(Matt.7:25). Helaman teaches us; if we build our lives upon the rock or sure foundation we cannot fail (Hel.

5:12). Remember truth is one eternal round. All truth fits perfectly together like a circle. When we memorize key scriptures (truths) we are placing in our minds jewels which can be used at will. These jewels will change our behavior in a very positive way. They can be accessed at will. We live in a very negative world (2 Tim.3:2-7) for the most part: by neglecting to fill our minds with positive things, "by default" we will fall into that state of mind. It takes desire and "persistent commitment" to rise above the status quo and live as Heavenly Father desires us to live. As we study, ponder and pray on true principles we are destined for peace, joy and happiness. For us to receive a "fullness of joy" is the purpose of our journey. We can receive our fondest dreams, as we work out our destiny using Truth (Matt. 6:33). The gospel of "Jesus Christ" is TRUTH. His way is the only way. His plan is given to all who desire to receive it (Matt.6:23). The Church of Jesus Christ of Latter Day Saints has the authority, the ordinance's, the covenants delegated from Heaven necessary for one to receive their greatest potential. Each of us have the potential to receive all the Father has. God is no respecter of persons. It is my solemn testimony, through "faith in Jesus Christ" revelation from Heaven is alive and well today and all who desire it and will "do" what is necessary to receive it, will receive it, for God is no respecter of persons. We are all his children, he loves us all, he desires all to have peace joy and happiness now and receive "fullness of joy" for eternity. Faith in Jesus Christ is the only way this can happen.

www.ingramcontent.com/pod-product-compliance
Lightning Source LLC
LaVergne TN
LVHW051225070526
838200LV00057B/4612